The Practice Toolkit

Lisa Reidsema, LMHC

Craft Your Practice - The Practice Toolkit

Copyright © 2025 by Lisa Reidsema

All rights reserved.

No portion of this book may be reproduced in any form without written permission from the publisher or author, except as permitted by U.S. copyright law

Lisa Reidsema, LMHC

Table of Contents

Introduction
- How to Use This Toolkit 1

Section One: Foundations & Vision 3
- Your Personal Why 4
- Your Professional Why 6
- Aligning Personal & Professional Why 8
- Vision Mapping: Personal, Professional, and Long-Term 10
- Vision Map Grid 15
- Reflections 16

Section Two: Foundations & Vision 18
- Naming Your Practice (Brainstorm + Final Choice) 20
- Legal & Financial Foundations Checklists 22
- Startup Costs Worksheet 24
- Monthly Expenses Worksheet 26
- Office & Systems Setup 28
- Technology & HIPAA Compliance Checklist 30
- Reflections 31

Section Three: Financial Tools 33
- Session Fee Calculator (Part 1) 34
- Session Fee Calculator (Part 2) 36
- Income Goals Worksheet 38
- Insurance & Credentialing Tracker 39
- Reimbursement Rate Log 40
- Accounts Receivable Tracker 41
- **Ongoing Financial Tracking** 43
    - 12 Monthly Income & Expense Trackers 44
    - 4 Quarterly Insurance/Payment Review Logs 56

Craft Your Practice - The Practice Toolkit

Lisa Reidsema, LMHC

Table of Contents

Section Four: Client Experience 61
- Ideal Caseload Worksheets 62
- Mapping the Client Journey 64
- Client Journey Map (Couples) 67
- Client Journey Map (Groups) 68
- Telehealth Policy (Template) 69
- Payment Agreement (Template) 70
- Cancellation & No-Show Policy (Template) 71
- Sliding Scale Agreement (Template) 72
- Emergency Contact Information (Template) 73
- Court Appearance Policy (Template) 74
- Reflections + Notes 75

Section Five: Growth & Marketing 79
- Marketing Brainstorm Worksheets 80
- Marketing Plan Worksheet 82
- Monthly Marketing Trackers (Core + Extended 12 Months) 88
- Website & Online Presence Checklist 100
- Networking & Referral Trackers 101
- Social Media Content Planners 104
- Marketing Reflections + Notes 107

Section Six: Sustainability & Reflection 109
- Weekly Self-Check Worksheets 110
- Burnout Prevention Plan 114
- Quarterly Reviews 115
- Year-End Reflection 120
- Final Notes 122

Craft Your Practice - The Practice Toolkit

Lisa Reidsema, LMHC

Introduction

How to Use This Toolkit

Welcome to the **Craft Your Practice Toolkit**. This workbook was designed to give you practical tools, worksheets, and templates to build and sustain your private practice. Think of it as both a guide and a companion—you'll return to these pages again and again as your practice grows.

Here's how to get the most out of it:

- **Start where you are.**
  You don't need to complete this workbook in order. Use the sections that feel most relevant right now—whether that's setting up your office, clarifying your fees, or mapping your marketing.

- **Write directly in the pages.**
  This book is meant to be used. Grab a pen or pencil, jot down your ideas, and don't be afraid to make a mess—clarity comes through writing and reflection.

- **Repeat and revisit.**
  Many worksheets appear in duplicate or as monthly/quarterly planners. These are intentional. Your vision, finances, and client systems will evolve over time, and these pages will help you track that growth.

- **Use the templates as a starting point.**
  The included policies and forms are samples. Adapt them to fit your voice, your practice, and your clients.

- **Pause for reflection.**
  At the end of each section, you'll find space for notes and self-reflection. Use these to capture insights, challenges, or next steps.

- **Give yourself permission.**
  Building a private practice is not a one-time project—it's an ongoing process. Allow yourself to experiment, shift, and keep crafting the practice that works for you.

This is your workbook. Make it your own.

Craft Your Practice - The Practice Toolkit

Lisa Reidsema, LMHC

Section One: Foundations & Vision

Before you set up the nuts and bolts of your practice, it's essential to ground yourself in your values, your "why," and your bigger vision. These exercises will guide you toward clarity and alignment.

Personal Why Worksheet

Why did you become a therapist? What parts of your story have shaped your decision to open a private practice?

_____
_____
_____
_____
_____
_____
_____
_____

- **Prompt One:** The personal experiences that led me here...

_____
_____
_____
_____
_____
_____
_____
_____

Lisa Reidsema, LMHC

Personal Why Worksheet

- **Prompt Two:** The values I want my practice to reflect are...

_____
_____
_____
_____
_____
_____
_____
_____
_____

- **Prompt Three:** When my practice is aligned with my values, I feel...

_____
_____
_____
_____
_____
_____
_____
_____
_____

Professional Why Worksheet

Beyond your personal story, what professional goals are you hoping private practice will help you achieve?

_____
_____
_____
_____
_____
_____
_____
_____
_____

- **Prompt One:** The impact I want to make on clients...

_____
_____
_____
_____
_____
_____
_____
_____

Lisa Reidsema, LMHC

Professional Why Worksheet

- **Prompt Two:** The professional lifestyle I want to create (schedule, income, balance)...

- **Prompt Three:** My long-term career goals include...

Aligning Personal & Professional Why

- What themes do you see in your answers from the last few pages?

_____
_____
_____
_____
_____
_____

- Where do your personal and professional "whys" overlap?

_____
_____
_____
_____

- Where do they differ?

_____
_____
_____
_____

Lisa Reidsema, LMHC

Aligning Personal & Professional Why

- **Prompt One:** The thread that ties my personal and professional whys together is…

- **Prompt Two:** I know I'm living my "why" when…

Craft Your Practice - The Practice Toolkit

Vision Mapping: Personal, Professional, & Long-Term

Why did you become a therapist? What parts of your story have shaped your decision to open a private practice?

- **Personal Vision** – the lifestyle you want

_____
_____
_____
_____
_____
_____
_____
_____
_____

- **Professional Vision** – the impact and reputation you want

_____
_____
_____
_____
_____
_____
_____
_____
_____

Vision Mapping: Personal, Professional, & Long-Term

- **Longterm Vision** – where you want to be in 5–10 years

Personal Vision Worksheet

Personal Vision: My Ideal Day
Imagine a day in your future practice. Walk through it hour by hour.

- Morning:
  _____
  _____
  _____
  _____

- Midday:
  _____
  _____
  _____
  _____

- Afternoon:
  _____
  _____
  _____
  _____

- Evening:
  _____
  _____
  _____
  _____

Lisa Reidsema, LMHC

Professional Vision Worksheet

Professional Vision: How I Serve Clients

- **Prompt One:** The clients I most want to serve are...

_____
_____
_____
_____
_____
_____
_____

- **Prompt Two:** The outcomes I hope to see in my clients are...

_____
_____
_____
_____
_____
_____
_____

- **Prompt Three:** My practice will be recognized for...

_____
_____
_____
_____
_____
_____

Long-Term Vision Worksheet

Looking Ahead: 5–10 Year Vision

- **Prompt One:** In 5 years, my practice will..

_____
_____
_____
_____
_____
_____

- **Prompt Two:** In 10 years, my career will...

_____
_____
_____
_____
_____
_____

- **Prompt Three:** The legacy I want to leave is...

_____
_____
_____
_____
_____

Vision Map Grid

	Vision Statement	Vision Statement	Vision Statement	Vision Statement
Personal				
Professional				
Long-Term				

Reflections On My Why & Vision

Use these pages to jot down insights, challenges, or themes that came up for you.

Reflections On My Why & Vision

Section Two: Practice Set-Up Essentials

This section walks you through the nuts and bolts of starting a private practice: naming it, legal and financial foundations, and creating systems that will support you for years to come.

Craft Your Practice - The Practice Toolkit

Name Brainstorm Grid

| Practice Name Idea | Pros | Cons | Availability Check
Domain/Social Media/LLC |
|---|---|---|---|
| | | | |
| | | | |
| | | | |
| | | | |
| | | | |

Choosing Your Practice Name

Which 1-2 names feel most aligned with my values and vision?

_____
_____

The name I am most drawn to is...

_____

This name reflects my vision because...

_____
_____
_____
_____

Next steps to make it official (check domain, file LLC, etc.):

_____
_____
_____
_____
_____
_____
_____

Legal & Financial Foundations Checklist: Part 1

- [ ] **Decide business structure (LLC, S-Corp, Sole Proprietor)**
  - [ ] File with state
  - [ ] Obtain EIN
  - [ ] Open business bank account
  - [ ] Get malpractice/liability insurance

Notes:

Lisa Reidsema, LMHC

Legal & Financial Foundations Checklist: Part 2

☐ **Choose accounting software or bookkeeper**

☐ Set up tax ID with IRS

☐ Track start-up costs

☐ Set aside funds for quarterly taxes

☐ Create budget categories (rent, utilities, CEUs, software, etc.)

Notes:

Budgeting Your Practice Start-Up

Expense Category	Estimated Cost	Actual Cost	Notes
Office Space			
Furniture & Decor			
Tech (computer, EMR, Zoom)			
Marketing & Website			
Legal & Insurance			
CEUs & Licensing			

Budgeting Your Practice Start-Up

Prompt: The total startup costs I expect are...

Notes:

Monthly Practice Budget

Expense Category	Estimated Cost	Actual Cost	Notes
Rent & Utilities			
Software & EMR			
Phone & Internet			
Marketing			
Continuing Education			
Miscellaneous			

Monthly Practice Budget

Prompt: My target monthly income needs to cover...

Office Setup Worksheet

- In-person, telehealth, or hybrid?

- Private office vs. sublet/shared space?

- How will clients contact you (phone, secure email, client portal)?

- What HIPAA-compliant systems do you need?

Office Setup Worksheet

Notes:

Technology & HIPAA Compliance Checklist

☐ **Choose HIPAA-compliant telehealth platform**

☐ Select EMR/EHR system

☐ Secure email & messaging

☐ Encrypted file storage

☐ Backup system in place

☐ Business Associate Agreements (BAAs) signed

Notes:

_____
_____
_____
_____
_____
_____
_____
_____
_____
_____
_____
_____

Reflections on Practice Foundations

- Which parts of setup feel easy?

- Which parts feel overwhelming?

- What support do I need?

Section Three: Financial Tools

Your practice is a business. To thrive, you need clarity around money — what's coming in, what's going out, and how you'll track it. This section gives you worksheets and templates to plan, manage, and grow financially.

Session Fee Calculator (Part 1)

Calculating Your Session Rate
- **Step One:** Write down your estimated monthly expenses.

_____
_____
_____
_____
_____
_____
_____
_____
_____

- **Step Two:** Write down the number of weekly sessions you want to hold.

_____
_____
_____
_____
_____
_____
_____
_____
_____

Lisa Reidsema, LMHC

Session Fee Calculator (Part 1)

- **Step Three:** Multiply weekly sessions × 4 to get monthly sessions.

- **Step Four:** Divide monthly expenses by monthly sessions.

This is your break-even fee.

Session Fee Calculator (Part 2)

Adding Profit + Taxes
- **Step One:** Add 25–30% to your break-even fee to cover taxes.

- **Step Two:** Add profit margin (savings, retirement, reinvestment).

Session Fee Calculator (Part 2)

- **Step Three:** Adjust for market rates in your area.

- **My final session fee is:**

  $

My Practice Income Goals

Goal Type	Amount	Notes
Office Space		
Comfortable Goal		
Dream Goal		

Prompt: The income level that feels most aligned with my vision is…

_____
_____
_____
_____
_____
_____
_____

Lisa Reidsema, LMHC

Insurance & Credentialing Tracker (Intro)

Tracking Insurance Applications

Insurance Tracker Table
Use this table to track which panels you've applied to, dates, and status.

Insurance Panel	Date Applied	Status *Pending/Approved/Denied*	Notes

Reimbursement Rate Log

Track Reimbursement Rates by Insurance

Insurance Panel	CPT Code	Rate	Notes

Prompt: The rates that best align with my financial needs are...

_____
_____
_____
_____

Lisa Reidsema, LMHC

Accounts Receivable Tracker

Outstanding Payments

Client Name	Date of Service	Amount Billed	Insurance Paid	Client Paid	Balance Owed

Reflections on Money & Practice

- How do I feel about setting my fee?

_____
_____
_____
_____
_____
_____
_____
_____

- What money stories or fears come up for me?

_____
_____
_____
_____
_____
_____
_____
_____
_____

Reflections on Money & Practice

- How will I remind myself that my work has value?

_____
_____
_____
_____
_____
_____
_____
_____
_____
_____
_____

Ongoing Financial Tracking

Now that you've calculated your session fee, income goals, and reimbursement rates, it's time to put your financial plan into practice. These pages give you space to track your practice finances throughout the year.

- **Monthly Income & Expenses Trackers**
  Record income, expenses, and balances each month to stay on top of cash flow.
- **Quarterly Review Logs**
  Review insurance payments, claims, and outstanding balances every 3 months.

Use these tools to spot trends, adjust as needed, and keep your practice financially healthy.

January • Income & Expenses

Category	Income	Expenses	Balance	Notes
Client Sessions				
Insurance				
Workshops/ Other				
Office Costs				
Marketing				
Continuing Ed				

• **Prompt:** My financial win this month was...

_____

_____

_____

_____

_____

_____

_____

February • Income & Expenses

Category	Income	Expenses	Balance	Notes
Client Sessions				
Insurance				
Workshops/ Other				
Office Costs				
Marketing				
Continuing Ed				

- **Prompt:** My financial win this month was...

_____
_____
_____
_____
_____
_____
_____

March • Income & Expenses

Category	Income	Expenses	Balance	Notes
Client Sessions				
Insurance				
Workshops/ Other				
Office Costs				
Marketing				
Continuing Ed				

• **Prompt:** My financial win this month was...

_____
_____
_____
_____
_____
_____

April • Income & Expenses

Category	Income	Expenses	Balance	Notes
Client Sessions				
Insurance				
Workshops/Other				
Office Costs				
Marketing				
Continuing Ed				

- **Prompt:** My financial win this month was...

_____
_____
_____
_____
_____
_____
_____

May • Income & Expenses

Category	Income	Expenses	Balance	Notes
Client Sessions				
Insurance				
Workshops/ Other				
Office Costs				
Marketing				
Continuing Ed				

• **Prompt:** My financial win this month was...

_____
_____
_____
_____
_____
_____
_____

June • Income & Expenses

Category	Income	Expenses	Balance	Notes
Client Sessions				
Insurance				
Workshops/ Other				
Office Costs				
Marketing				
Continuing Ed				

- **Prompt:** My financial win this month was...

_____
_____
_____
_____
_____
_____
_____

July • Income & Expenses

Category	Income	Expenses	Balance	Notes
Client Sessions				
Insurance				
Workshops/ Other				
Office Costs				
Marketing				
Continuing Ed				

• **Prompt:** My financial win this month was...

_____
_____
_____
_____
_____
_____
_____

August • Income & Expenses

Category	Income	Expenses	Balance	Notes
Client Sessions				
Insurance				
Workshops/ Other				
Office Costs				
Marketing				
Continuing Ed				

- **Prompt:** My financial win this month was...

_____
_____
_____
_____
_____
_____
_____

September • Income & Expenses

Category	Income	Expenses	Balance	Notes
Client Sessions				
Insurance				
Workshops/ Other				
Office Costs				
Marketing				
Continuing Ed				

• **Prompt:** My financial win this month was...

_____
_____
_____
_____
_____
_____
_____

Lisa Reidsema, LMHC

October · Income & Expenses

Category	Income	Expenses	Balance	Notes
Client Sessions				
Insurance				
Workshops/ Other				
Office Costs				
Marketing				
Continuing Ed				

- **Prompt:** My financial win this month was…

_____
_____
_____
_____
_____
_____
_____

November • Income & Expenses

Category	Income	Expenses	Balance	Notes
Client Sessions				
Insurance				
Workshops/ Other				
Office Costs				
Marketing				
Continuing Ed				

- **Prompt:** My financial win this month was...

_____
_____
_____
_____
_____
_____
_____

December · Income & Expenses

Category	Income	Expenses	Balance	Notes
Client Sessions				
Insurance				
Workshops/ Other				
Office Costs				
Marketing				
Continuing Ed				

- **Prompt:** My financial win this month was...

_____
_____
_____
_____
_____
_____
_____

Craft Your Practice - The Practice Toolkit

Quarter One • Insurance/Payment Review Log

Insurance Panel	Clients Seen	Claims Submitted	Amount Paid	Outstanding
Client Sessions				
Insurance				
Workshops/ Other				
Office Costs				
Marketing				
Continuing Ed				

- **Prompt:** My financial win this quarter was...

_____
_____
_____
_____
_____
_____

Lisa Reidsema, LMHC

Quarter Two • Insurance/Payment Review Log

Insurance Panel	Clients Seen	Claims Submitted	Amount Paid	Outstanding
Client Sessions				
Insurance				
Workshops/ Other				
Office Costs				
Marketing				
Continuing Ed				

- **Prompt:** My financial win this quarter was...

_____
_____
_____
_____
_____
_____

Quarter Three • Insurance/Payment Review Log

Insurance Panel	Clients Seen	Claims Submitted	Amount Paid	Outstanding
Client Sessions				
Insurance				
Workshops/ Other				
Office Costs				
Marketing				
Continuing Ed				

• **Prompt:** My financial win this quarter was…

_____
_____
_____
_____
_____
_____
_____

Quarter Four • Insurance/Payment Review Log

Insurance Panel	Clients Seen	Claims Submitted	Amount Paid	Outstanding
Client Sessions				
Insurance				
Workshops/ Other				
Office Costs				
Marketing				
Continuing Ed				

• **Prompt:** My financial win this quarter was...

_____
_____
_____
_____
_____
_____
_____

Section Four: Client Experience

Your clients' experience begins before the first session and continue through every interaction. This section helps you clarify who you serve, how you want them to feel, and what systems support a smooth client journey.

Ideal Caseload Worksheet • Who I want to work with

• **Prompt One:** The demographics I'm most drawn to serve are...

_____
_____
_____
_____
_____
_____
_____

• **Prompt Two:** The issues or specialties I most enjoy working with are...

_____
_____
_____
_____
_____

• **Prompt Three:** My preferred session times (mornings, evenings, weekends) are...

_____
_____
_____
_____

Ideal Caseload Worksheet • Caseload Structure

- Number of sessions per week I want to hold: _____

- Number of sessions per day that feels sustainable: _____

- Maximum total caseload I want to maintain: _____

- **Prompt:** My ideal caseload would give me...

_____
_____
_____
_____
_____
_____
_____
_____
_____
_____
_____
_____
_____

Craft Your Practice - The Practice Toolkit

Extended Client Tools

You've identified your ideal caseload and mapped the client journey. The following pages provide extra tools and templates to support you as you refine your practice. Use them to track different service types, clarify policies, and adapt forms for your unique needs.

- **Client Journey Maps**
  Use additional templates to track processes for individuals, couples, or groups.

- **Policy Templates**
  Customize telehealth, sliding scale, and emergency contact forms.

- **Notes Pages**
  Capture reflections about your client experience and systems.

Lisa Reidsema, LMHC

Mapping the Client Journey: Page 1

Every practice has a flow — from referral to intake to discharge. Design your process.

Client Journey Flow (Part One)

Step	Action	Who Is Responsible	Notes
Referral Received			
Intake Call			
Paperwork Sent			
First Session			

Mapping the Client Journey: Page 2

Client Journey Flow (Part Two)

Step	Action	Who Is Responsible	Notes
Ongoing Sessions			
Progress Review			
Termination/ Discharge			
Follow Up/ Referral			

- Notes

_____

_____

_____

Lisa Reidsema, LMHC

Client Journey Map: Couples

Step	Action	Who Is Responsible	Notes
Inquiry			
Intake Call			
Joint Intake Session			
Ongoing Sessions			
Termination/ Discharge			

- **Prompt:** The biggest differences in my couples process are...

_____

_____

_____

Client Journey Map: Groups

Step	Action	Who Is Responsible	Notes
Recruitment			
Intake Process			
Group Start			
Weekly Sessions			
Closing Session			

- **Prompt:** The most important thing to track in groups is...

_____

_____

_____

Lisa Reidsema, LMHC

Telehealth Policy: Template

Telehealth Policy

- Sessions are conducted via secure, HIPAA-compliant video platform.
- Clients must ensure they have a private, quiet space for sessions.
- Clients are responsible for ensuring internet connection and technology access.
- In case of technical issues, sessions may be conducted by phone.

Client Acknowledgment Signature: _____

Notes for customization:

_____
_____
_____
_____
_____
_____
_____
_____

Payment Agreement: Template

Payment Agreement

- Session fee: $ _____ per session.

- Payment is due at the time of service unless otherwise agreed.

- Accepted payment methods _____

- Outstanding balances must be paid before scheduling new sessions.

Client Acknowledgment Signature: _____

Notes for customization:

_____

_____

_____

_____

_____

_____

_____

Lisa Reidsema, LMHC

Cancellation & No-Show Policy: Template

Cancellation & No-Show Policy

- Sessions must be canceled with at least 24 hours' notice.
- Sessions canceled with less notice will be charged at the full session rate.
- Exceptions may be made in case of emergencies.

Client Acknowledgment Signature: _____

Notes for customization:

_____
_____
_____
_____
_____
_____
_____

Sliding Scale Agreement: Template

Sliding Scale Agreement

- Standard session fee: $ _____

- Adjusted sliding scale: $ _____

- This agreement is reviewed every 6 months.

Client Acknowledgment Signature: _____

Notes for customization:

_____

_____

_____

_____

_____

_____

_____

Emergency Contact Form: Template

Emergency Contact Form

Client Name: _____

- Primary Emergency Contact:

    Name: _____

    Relationship: _____

    Phone: _____

- Secondary Emergency Contact:

    Name: _____

    Relationship: _____

    Phone: _____

Notes for customization:

_____
_____
_____
_____
_____
_____
_____

Craft Your Practice - The Practice Toolkit

Court Appearance Policy: Template

Court Appearance Policy

- Court appearances are billed at $ _____ per hour (including preparation and travel time).
- Minimum fee: $ _____
- Additional costs (travel, parking, waiting time) may apply.

Client Acknowledgment Signature: _____

Notes for customization:

_____

_____

_____

_____

_____

_____

_____

Lisa Reidsema, LMHC

Reflections & Notes: Client Experience

How do I want clients to feel when they work with me?

_____
_____
_____
_____
_____
_____
_____
_____

What boundaries or policies protect my time and energy?

_____
_____
_____
_____
_____
_____
_____
_____
_____
_____

Reflections & Notes: Client Experience

Where could I simplify my client systems?

Reflections & Notes: Client Experience

Use this space to jot down ideas, concerns, or adjustments you want to make to your client experience.

Section Five: Growth & Marketing

Your practice can't thrive if no one knows it exists. This section helps you create a simple marketing plan, track your efforts, and build referral relationships in ways that feel authentic and sustainable.

Marketing Brainstorm Worksheet: Part 1

- **Prompt:** Brainstorm all the ways you might market your practice. Don't edit, just write freely.

Lisa Reidsema, LMHC

Marketing Brainstorm Worksheet: Part 2

- Now categorize your ideas.

Method	Audience	Cost	Time Commitment	ROI Potential
Website				
Psychology Today				
Social Media				
Networking				
Workshops/ CEUs				

Marketing Plan Worksheet

- **Three Marketing Actions I Will Focus On:**

    1. _____

        Timeline _____

    2. _____

        Timeline _____

    3. _____

        Timeline _____

Marketing Plan Worksheet

- **Prompt:** I chose these three actions because...

Monthly Marketing Tracker: Page 1

Month	Marketing Action	Cost	Time Spent	Notes

Monthly Marketing Tracker: Page 2

Month	Marketing Action	Cost	Time Spent	Notes

Extended Growth & Marketing Tools

You've brainstormed your marketing ideas and built a starter plan. The following pages give you monthly trackers and planning tools to keep your marketing consistent, focused, and effective

- **Monthly Marketing Trackers**
  Record actions, costs, and outcomes each month.

- **Social Media Content Planners**
  Organize your online presence with simple prompts.

- **Notes Pages**
  Capture insights, patterns, and fresh marketing ideas.

January • Marketing Tracker

Marketing Action	Cost	Time Spent	New Clients or Leads	Notes

- **Prompt:** The marketing action that worked best this month was...

_____
_____
_____
_____
_____
_____

February • Marketing Tracker

Marketing Action	Cost	Time Spent	New Clients or Leads	Notes

- **Prompt:** The marketing action that worked best this month was…

_____
_____
_____
_____
_____
_____

March • Marketing Tracker

Marketing Action	Cost	Time Spent	New Clients or Leads	Notes

• **Prompt:** The marketing action that worked best this month was...

_____
_____
_____
_____
_____
_____

April • Marketing Tracker

Marketing Action	Cost	Time Spent	New Clients or Leads	Notes

- **Prompt:** The marketing action that worked best this month was...

_____
_____
_____
_____
_____
_____

May • Marketing Tracker

Marketing Action	Cost	Time Spent	New Clients or Leads	Notes

- **Prompt:** The marketing action that worked best this month was...

_____
_____
_____
_____
_____
_____

June • Marketing Tracker

Marketing Action	Cost	Time Spent	New Clients or Leads	Notes

- **Prompt:** The marketing action that worked best this month was...

_____
_____
_____
_____
_____
_____

Craft Your Practice - The Practice Toolkit

July • Marketing Tracker

Marketing Action	Cost	Time Spent	New Clients or Leads	Notes

• **Prompt:** The marketing action that worked best this month was…

_____
_____
_____
_____
_____

Lisa Reidsema, LMHC

August • Marketing Tracker

Marketing Action	Cost	Time Spent	New Clients or Leads	Notes

- **Prompt:** The marketing action that worked best this month was...

_____
_____
_____
_____
_____
_____

Craft Your Practice - The Practice Toolkit

September • Marketing Tracker

Marketing Action	Cost	Time Spent	New Clients or Leads	Notes

• **Prompt:** The marketing action that worked best this month was...

_____
_____
_____
_____
_____

Lisa Reidsema, LMHC

October • Marketing Tracker

Marketing Action	Cost	Time Spent	New Clients or Leads	Notes

• **Prompt:** The marketing action that worked best this month was...

_____
_____
_____
_____
_____
_____

November • Marketing Tracker

Marketing Action	Cost	Time Spent	New Clients or Leads	Notes

- **Prompt:** The marketing action that worked best this month was...

_____
_____
_____
_____
_____

December • Marketing Tracker

Marketing Action	Cost	Time Spent	New Clients or Leads	Notes

• **Prompt:** The marketing action that worked best this month was...

_____
_____
_____
_____
_____
_____

Website & Online Presence Checklist

☐ Purchase Domain

☐ Build simple practice website

☐ Create professional email address

☐ Set up Psychology Today profile (or similar directory)

☐ Establish Google Business listing

☐ Choose 1-2 social media platforms to maintain

Prompt: The online presence tasks I want to prioritize first are...

_____
_____
_____
_____
_____
_____
_____
_____
_____
_____
_____

Networking & Referral Tracker: Page 1

Referral Source	Date Connected	Type *Therapist, Doctor, Community*	Follow-Up Needed	Notes

Networking & Referral Tracker: Page 2

Referral Source	Date Connected	Type *Therapist, Doctor, Community*	Follow-Up Needed	Notes

Networking & Referral Tracker: Page 3

Referral Source	Date Connected	Type *Therapist, Doctor, Community*	Follow-Up Needed	Notes

Social Media Content Planner

Week of _____

- Post Idea 1:

  _____
  _____

- Post Idea 2:

  _____
  _____

- Blog/Video Topic:

  _____
  _____

- Engagement Strategy:

  _____
  _____
  _____
  _____
  _____

Social Media Content Planner

Notes:

Marketing Reflections

- What strategies brought the most new clients?

- What strategies drained time without results?

Marketing Reflections

- What would I like to try next?

Lisa Reidsema, LMHC

Section Six: Sustainability & Reflection

Building a practice is not just about clients and income, it's also about you. These worksheets help you stay resourced, prevent burnout, and reflect on your growth.

Weekly Self-Check Worksheet

- What's working in my practice this week?

___

- What feels challenging or draining?

___

Lisa Reidsema, LMHC

Weekly Self-Check Worksheet

- One small thing I can do to feel more supported is...

_____
_____
_____
_____
_____
_____
_____
_____
_____

- This week I give myself permission to...

_____
_____
_____
_____
_____
_____
_____
_____
_____

Weekly Self-Check Worksheet

(Duplicate for on going use)

- What's working in my practice this week?

___

- What feels challenging or draining?

___

Lisa Reidsema, LMHC

Weekly Self-Check Worksheet

- One small thing I can do to feel more supported is...

_____
_____
_____
_____
_____
_____
_____
_____
_____

- This week I give myself permission to...

_____
_____
_____
_____
_____
_____
_____
_____
_____

Burnout Prevention Plan

Warning Signs of Burnout for Me

Support Systems I Can Lean On

Lisa Reidsema, LMHC

Burnout Prevention Plan

My Prevention Strategies

- Boundaries I will keep around my time...

_____
_____
_____
_____
_____
_____
_____

- Activities that restore my energy...

_____
_____
_____
_____
_____
_____

- My plan for vacations, breaks, or rest periods...

_____
_____
_____
_____
_____
_____

Quarterly Review: First Quarter

- My wins this quarter were...

_____
_____
_____
_____

- My wins this quarter were...

_____
_____
_____
_____

- Financial snapshot (income vs. expenses)

_____
_____

- My top 3 priorities for next quarter are:

_____
_____
_____
_____
_____

Lisa Reidsema, LMHC

Quarterly Review: Second Quarter

- My wins this quarter were...
  _____
  _____
  _____
  _____

- My wins this quarter were...
  _____
  _____
  _____
  _____

- Financial snapshot (income vs. expenses)
  _____
  _____

- My top 3 priorities for next quarter are:
  _____
  _____
  _____
  _____
  _____

Quarterly Review: Third Quarter

- My wins this quarter were...

_____
_____
_____
_____

- My wins this quarter were...

_____
_____
_____
_____

- Financial snapshot (income vs. expenses)

_____
_____

- My top 3 priorities for next quarter are:

_____
_____
_____
_____
_____

Lisa Reidsema, LMHC

Quarterly Review: Fourth Quarter

- My wins this quarter were...
___
___
___
___

- My wins this quarter were...
___
___
___
___

- Financial snapshot (income vs. expenses)
___
___

- My top 3 priorities for next quarter are:
___
___
___
___
___
___

Year-end Reflection

- **Prompt One:** The accomplishments I am most proud of are...

_____
_____
_____
_____
_____
_____
_____
_____

- **Prompt Two:** The challenges I overcame were...

_____
_____
_____
_____
_____
_____
_____
_____

Year-end Reflection

- **Prompt Three:** The biggest lesson I will carry forward is...

_____
_____
_____
_____
_____
_____
_____
_____
_____
_____

- **Prompt Four:** My goals for the next year are...

_____
_____
_____
_____
_____
_____
_____
_____
_____
_____

Final Notes & Insights

Use these pages for any last reflections, ideas, or reminders for next year.

- You already have the skills and wisdom to help your clients.
- This toolkit is here to support you as you shape the *business* side of your practice.
- Every step, no matter how small, moves you closer to the vision you imagined in these pages.
- Your practice will grow, shift, and evolve, and so will you. Come back to these worksheets whenever you need clarity, encouragement, or a fresh perspective.
- You are not just building a practice. You are crafting a life, a livelihood, and a legacy.

Keep crafting. Keep going. The work you're doing matters

_____
_____
_____
_____
_____
_____
_____
_____
_____
_____
_____
_____
_____

Final Notes & Insights

Craft Your Practice - The Practice Toolkit

Lisa Reidsema, LMHC

About the author

Lisa Reidsema, LMHC is a licensed therapist, author, and educator with a passion for helping clinicians design sustainable and fulfilling private practices.

Before becoming a therapist, Lisa spent many years as an educator, where she developed her love for teaching, mentoring, and making complex topics feel approachable. She later built and managed a thriving group practice before shifting to a more personalized, values-driven approach, which deepened her focus on trauma work and helping others grow their own businesses with clarity and confidence.

Through **Craft Your Practice**, Lisa now guides therapists step-by-step through the process of building, organizing, and sustaining a private practice. Her books, workbooks, courses, and coaching are designed to give clinicians practical tools and the encouragement they need to turn their vision into reality

 Discover more resources at: www.craftyourpractice.com

Also Available from Craft Your Practice

Take the next step in crafting a private practice that works for you.

Craft Your Practice: *A Guide to Building a Personalized Private Practice*

Your foundational guide to starting and shaping a practice that aligns with your values and vision.

Craft Your Practice: A Companion Workbook

A hands-on companion filled with exercises, prompts, and space to bring your ideas into action.

Craft Your Practice: Credentialing, Insurance, and Getting Paid

This guide provides step-by-step instructions for credentialing, contracting, and creating efficient billing systems to ensure you get paid.

The Therapist's Toolkit

Forms, policies, and ready-to-use templates that save you time and help you run your practice smoothly.

Online Courses (Coming Soon!)

Step-by-step video lessons that expand on the book and workbook, including:
Building Your Practice from the Ground Up
Credentialing, Insurance, and Getting Paid

Discover more resources at: www.craftyourpractice.com

www.ingramcontent.com/pod-product-compliance
Lightning Source LLC
Chambersburg PA
CBHW080550030426
42337CB00024B/4822